EPSOM
A Pictorial History

Pub by J. N. Collingwood Epsom

The Clock Tower, symbol of prosperous Victorian Epsom, was built in 1848 beside the town pond, which was drained six years later. In this view of 1860, people are promenading where the cows of the medieval village used to drink. J. N. Collingwood, who published this engraving, gave pride of place to his library and bookbinders on the left. The site, nos. 111 - 113, is now occupied by Lester Bowden. Next to it is Barnard the pastrycook and confectioner, where Mrs. Beeton learnt her skills.

EPSOM
A Pictorial History

Trevor White
and
Jeremy Harte

Phillimore

1992

Published by
PHILLIMORE & CO. LTD.,
Shopwyke Hall, Chichester, Sussex

ISBN 0 85033 841 1

Printed and bound in Great Britain by
BIDDLES LTD.,
Guildford, Surrey

To Hazel and Stuart Wynn Jones
distinguished and diligent artists

List of Illustrations

Frontispiece: The High Street, 1860

Acknowledgements

Acknowledgements and very sincere thanks to Peter and Margaret Gamble at Kall Kwik printing and to Surrey County Library staff at both Epsom and Ewell.

Appreciation to Heather Pitt, Jane Morris, Leslie Bond, Michael Everett, Maurice Giles, Peter Lemon and Michael Staples.

The interior photograph of the Odeon cinema was supplied by the Royal Commission on the Historical Monuments of Britain.

Ian Allan Ltd. supplied photograph 108.

Great appreciation is due to many organisations that have provided material for this book: these include Ebbisham Sports Club, Epsom Bowling Club and the Royal Automobile Club at Woodcote.

It has not been possible to quote sources for all statements made in this book, but copies with full references have been deposited at the Epsom and Ewell libraries.

Introduction

In the British Museum there is a Saxon pendant that was found some years ago by an Epsom labourer. A golden mount ornamented with beadwork surrounds a garnet cameo carved with the bust of a bearded man: one of the three kings, perhaps, imported from the east. The jewel is Mediterranean, the setting is native work. It would be pleasant to think of this adorning the lady Ebbi after whom our town, Ebbi's ham, has been named, and who has been identified by local romance with a saint or queen. Certainly the jewel proves that there was seventh-century settlement in the area. In north-east Surrey, at the foot of the Downs, there is a string of villages called *ham*, from Effingham through Bookham to Cheam. Epsom, like the others, lies on the borderline where the soft chalk hills meet the intractable London clay. Between the two there is a plateau of gravelly soil, deposited by a river in more recent geological ages.

The parish church, dedicated to St Martin of Tours, was built on a chalk knoll at the base of the Downs, while the houses and gardens of the hamlet lay on either side of Church Street. Here they had an easy water supply, for winter streams called the Earthbourne welled up at the junction of chalk and clay. In 933 the hero-king Athelstan confirmed the settlement as the property of Chertsey Abbey.

Domesday Book records 38 peasant households cultivating the thin chalky soil south and east of the church. Four or five hundred acres were divided into strips over an area known to later generations as Smith Hatch Field from the hatch (a gate) through which East Street left the village and headed out over the common fields. Along this route waggons travelled laden with corn, making their way to the Lower Mill at Ewell, another Chertsey Abbey property. On the gravelly soil to the north of the common fields, the monks had established a home farm – Epsom Court – tended by six slaves. To the west, three-quarters of the manor was an unreclaimed oakwood, under which a herd of 200 swine snuffled for acorns. At that time, there were more pigs than people in Epsom.

Over the next century, young labourers cleared land for themselves on this waste ground. By 1202, a second hamlet called Woodcote had been built around a triangular green at the edge of the wood. Woodcote Field extended to the western border of the chalk lands, divided from Smith Hatch Field on the east by a trackway – now Rifle Butts Alley. In 1155 the monks created a hunting park by enclosing the south-western corner of the parish just beyond Woodcote. On the Chessington side, an estate of two square miles, mostly on the heavy clay soil, had been granted as a subordinate manor to tenants who ungratefully gave it the name of Horton, 'dirty farm'.

When the village prospered, the nave of the church was rebuilt in Early English style, and in the 1280s the rector – Roger of the Grove – renovated the chancel in a matching style. At the same time, the abbey's planners attempted to make Epsom into a formal settlement. Along the road from London to Leatherhead (now the western High Street) surveyors laid out a double row of building plots called Ebbisham Street, backing onto meadowland and fronting a large, egg-shaped pond dug partly for the benefit of cattle and partly to drain some water from the new houses.

The planned growth of the village came to an end with the Black Death in 1348. Outlying settlements suffered the most. The hamlet of Langley Bottom, established in the populous early 13th century, was wiped out. It was not until six centuries later that it was rebuilt and given the more genteel name of Langley Vale. But another peripheral community called At Clay survived in the area of West Hill and Stamford Green. By the 15th century, when St Martin's was being dignified with a flint tower, the new district had prospered and acquired a chapel of its own on the eastern side of Stamford Pond.

By 1496 Epsom had over 60 houses, spread out evenly between the settlements of Church Street, Ebbisham Street, Woodcote and At Clay. The farmhouse at Epsom Court was rebuilt in the early 16th century, and after the dissolution of Chertsey Abbey it passed, together with the manorial rights over Epsom, into the hands of the Mynn family of Horton. They rejected the timber-framed grange at Epsom Court and the moated manor at Horton in favour of Woodcote Park, where a Tudor mansion was built in the old hunting-ground. The enterprising tenants of At Clay had discovered the brick-making properties of their subsoil – Epsom bricks were already in demand at Croydon in 1541 – so there was no shortage of materials. Next to the park another mansion called Durdans had replaced a 14th-century farm.

The waste ground which formerly dominated the manor was now reduced to some four hundred acres, now known as Epsom Common. Here, sheep came off the Downs to graze between November and March, while geese, pigs and cattle remained throughout the year. It was (according to tradition) one of these cows which, in about 1620, was responsible for Epsom's greatness. In a dry summer, the only water available had welled up in one of her footprints. More water sprung up when her master, Henry Wicker, dug a hole at the site. Put off bythe smell of magnesium sulphate, she refused to drink from it: but human beings, less squeamish and more hypochondriac, discovered it had laxative effects. Within ten years, visitors from this country and abroad were coming to drink up to 12 pints of the stuff. By 1662, when the Dutch traveller William Schellinks sketched the well, Epsom was 'a very famous and much visited place', although the converion of its farmhouses and cottages into lodgings was very superficial. Schellinks' travelling companion was woken at midnight by the commotion as a pig ran through the kitchen towards the bedrooms.

On a summer Sunday morning, East Street would be full of Londoners travelling over the fields to Epsom Common. By eight o'clock, when Samuel Pepys arrived at the Wells in July 1667, the place was crowded: and dotted around the wasteland were bushes, concealing those visitors who had been served with the laxative and were leaving the effects behind them. There was little ceremony involved. The well, surrounded by a low wall and a brick pavement, stood in a gloomy cottage adorned with an incongruous classical façade. Pepys took his wife back to the coach, which carried them to the *King's Head* (now Kings Shade Walk in the High Street). He disliked the room they were shown, but could do little about it as there was only one other hostelry, the *New Inn* in Dorking Road. Elizabeth Amus, the landlady of the

Kings Head, prospered enough from such guests to mint her own halfpennies for local use in 1667 and 1668.

Pepys only visited Epsom for the day, but others stayed for weeks on end. There was little to do in the village, and time was often filled up with sexual intrigues. 'If you were not monstrously lewd, the freedom of Epsom allows almost nothing to be scandalous', says a character in Shadwell's *Epsom Wells,* (1672). Sometimes the dissoluteness of the town became too much for neighbouring communities. By 1676 Box Hill had become a favourite venue for weekend outings. Uneasy duellists would wait here for their opponents in the morning mists, and little parties would adjourn in the evening to a small grotto, near which couples might find themselves conveniently lost among the trees. It was all too much for the hot-blooded Puritan youths of Dorking. A group of them (including the young Daniel Defoe) laid a trail of gunpowder in the grotto and blew it up, leaving the lovers of Epsom to pursue their happiness elsewhere.

Epsom had about a hundred houses in 1680, which was no great increase on its medieval population. But wealthy Londoners were growing tired of the smoke and noise, the fire and plague of their crowded city and looked to Surrey for relief. Since the 1560s at least, urban merchants had been buying up Epsom fields and cottages as part of their landed investments. Why not build a new home there?

The brickfield on the common had been enlarged in 1663 on somewhat uncommercial tenancy terms – 5s. a year to the poor, cheap bricks for the Lord of the Manor, and nothing to be allowed to injure cattle. Now it was to prove an inexhaustible womb of baroque architecture. Westgate House, Woodcote Grove, the Hylands, Woodcote Green House, the Old Vicarage and the Cedars all came out of this hole in the ground. From 1680 to 1720 Epsom bystanders could see the completion of a new mansion every other year. The old house at Durdans was pulled down and replaced by something more palatial, ornamented with curiosities from Nonsuch Palace. The demand for these new mansions brought skills and people into the local building trade, and workmen were soon also engaged in building places of leisure and entertainment for the ordinary visitors. To begin with, there had been nowhere to go but the alehouses. It was at one of these that the dissolute Earl of Rochester sat drinking with some friends in 1676. Epsom had a band of fiddlers, versatile characters who could play dance music or serenade the lady of your choice: for a small fee they would go away altogether. Rochester and his companions had waylaid some of these fiddlers and were tossing them in a blanket for refusing to play when 'a barber, upon the noise, going to see what was the matter, they seized upon him, and, to free himself from them, he offered to carry them to the handsomest woman in Epsom, and directed them to the constable's house, who demanding what they came for, they told him a whore and, he refusing to let them in, they broke open his doors and beat him very seriously'.

In the 1670s two bowling greens were laid out, one to the west of Fair Green and the other on a meadow called Phillips Close, where South Street left the High Street. Bowling greens usually belonged to the houses of the aristocracy – there was one at Durdans, and there had been one at Nonsuch.

The green in Phillips Close was flanked by a little row of shops, a sign of increasing trade soon followed by the establishment of a market in 1680. In 1692 two London goldsmiths developed the site with two buildings of unprecedented grandeur. The

New Tavern (now the National Counties Building Society) contained a row of shops – pastrycooks, milliners, importers of porcelain – flanking a central alley into which the carriages drove. Passengers would alight here and ascend the grand staircase to the tavern rooms, where dinner was served in the evening and the new pleasure of coffee was enjoyed during the day. The Assembly Room lay to the south, where a modern coffee-shop is now. On one side it was flanked by a colonnade and trees; on the other, window seats padded with cushions looked out over the bowling green. Here the gambling tables were cleared to make room for dancing at night.

These attractions were intended to rival improvements made on the Common by the Evelyn family in 1690. Now an Assembly Room 70 ft. long adjoined the well, lined with wainscoting on which visitors carved their names. Some ten years later a new inn was built in the centre of the town and sold to a cook called Henry North. The inn was called the *Black Spread Eagle* as a tribute to the Hapsburgs whose coat of arms was an eagle and from whose Rhineland North acquired his best wine. Finally in 1707 John Livingstone, who had been an apothecary in Epsom since 1690, developed the land to the west of the High Street. He laid out a third bowling green, a garden and a grove of trees, built more shops and a third Assembly Room, and opened a new well for those who still liked to drink Epsom waters. The establishment was known as the New Wells, in rivalry with the Old Wells on the Common.

For perhaps 20 years Epsom offered a full range of diversions. However, by 1730 the town suddenly lost popularity.

> Bath's springs next in fashion came rapidly on,
> And outdid by far, whate'er Epsom had done.

At the same time, the great building boom came to an end, and contractors began to sell off the land which they had bought as an investment. James Allwright became a tenant in the East Street house which he himself had built, and William Newman, who had been involved in erecting the Hookfield mansion, went bankrupt in 1725. After the construction of Maidstone House and Woodcote Hall, Epsom had no more new mansions.

It was thought that the spa had declined when the old wells on the Common were abandoned in favour of the pleasures to be found in the town. Attempts were made to revive interest in the waters in 1754 and again in 1769 but without much success. The shops at the *New Tavern* were closed, and part of the grounds were leased to a blacksmith. Another blacksmith and a cooper had set up yards at the New Wells by 1770.

If the reputation of the waters had failed, Epsom still had its fine houses with which to attract the gentry. In the mid-century the town continued to provide employment for apothecaries and coffeemen, wig-makers, watch-menders and other trades unlikely to be found in a rural setting. The great houses, no longer in demand for Restoration rakes, acquired tenants of a more sober cast. John Brathwaite of Hookfield (a member of the gentry) 'exhibited a singular and uniform pattern of universal benevolence, for his only object was to do good'. According to the monument in St Martin's, 'the virtuous energies of his mind comprehended all those humanities and sympathies of which our nature in its best state is susceptible'. It is to be hoped that the Barbados slaves from whom he derived his income appreciated these good qualities.

The conditions in which the poor of Epsom lived were variable. The twelve widows, who were accommodated in the almshouses built in 1703 along East Street, at least had a home of their own. Others, less fortunate, were taken to the workhouse on the Dorking Road. Here a commission of 1779 found 'the children nearly in a state of nakedness, most part of them without stockings or shoes, dirty, lousey, and in a very wretched condition ... We found there Hugh Scriven a lunatic, partly naked, and chained, with the door open, hogs in the room, which might have destroyed him'.

By 1800 Epsom had over 400 houses, about one in ten the residence of a gentleman. However, several of them had fallen into disrepair, and the civic avenues of lime and elm trees were being felled. Some attempts were made by concerned residents to revive the place. The Congregational chapel in Church Street, which had been used as a barn for 20 years, was restored for worship in 1805. After a second period of decline, when most of the congregation defected to the little Bugby Chapel in Prospect Place, it was reopened in 1825. At the same time the medieval church of St Martin's was pulled down and rebuilt at a cost of £6,000, most of it borrowed on the security of the rates.

Commercial life picked up slowly. Seven coaches were expected each day from London on the Brighton route, stopping off at the extensive stables behind the *Spread Eagle*. Here auctions were held, and an upper room was set aside for freemasons to conduct their rites. The parish authorities met at the *Spread Eagle* and the *King's Head* to discharge their responsibilities for the state of the roads and the condition of the poor, while the magistrates convened at the *Albion*.

Meanwhile, the town was acquiring a new source of prosperity. Throughout the previous century, racing had taken place on the Downs, attracting spectators. The racing regulations of 1778 anticipated that people from London would come down to erect booths for the sale of liquor. The founding of the Derby two years later was meant to satisfy public demand for a shorter and more exciting race. In 1828 an entrepreneur from Doncaster called Charles Bluck leased land to build a grandstand. It was finished two years later after Bluck had been bought out by more reputable citizens. It came at the right time. Between 1825 and 1843 the crowd attracted to the Downs doubled in size to reach 128,000. Derby Day became an important social occasion as well as a sporting event. The throng on the hill included 'giants, dwarfs, peers, blacklegs ... Jews, jockies, persons equally intent on cheating and being cheated – gipsies capable of telling everybodies' fortune but their own – horses at full speed – a beautiful expanse of wooded country – St Pauls seen dim and indistinct as a shadow in the extreme distance'.

The popularity of the races created a problem, with traffic jams which could stretch seven or eight miles from the Downs. Now railway companies hoped to provide a solution. The London, Brighton and South Coast Railway ran a line through from Croydon and Ewell East in 1847, establishing their station in Upper High Street. The London and South Western were responsible for the line from Wimbledon through Ewell West, and in 1859 the two rivals agreed on joint operation of the track from the present Epsom Station to Ashtead. Trains did not come to Epsom Downs until 1865.

Epsom traders had been anxious for a railway. After the event there were to be doubts about the wisdom of progress, as the gentry abandoned High Street shops in favour of Piccadilly and Oxford Street, but in 1847 the sense of euphoria was still strong, and the Vestry chose the moment to rebuild the old Watch House. Built in the days of the spa, this stood beside the town pond and contained a fire engine little younger than itself. Butler & Hodge of London submitted a design for a new Clock Tower, 30 ft. higher than the old and imitating an Italian campanile in Victorian polychrome brick, which the Vestry approved unanimously.

Epsom now had 600 houses, but the town had not spread outwards over the century, so that accommodation was increasingly crowded. About a third of the properties were cheap weatherboarded designs. Because of the high water table, it was easy for cesspits to pollute the pumps; at the back of the *Albion* there were six privies and three wells within a few dozen yards of each other. As more houses were built, the average lifespan fell to forty years.

A local board of health was elected in 1850. They constructed sewers and drained the town pond, to the distress of some who remembered angling in it for goldfish, and the relief of others who recalled the dead dogs floating there. In 1853 they sank an artesian well off East Street which supplied 20 gallons a day to each inhabitant of Epsom.

The town was still small, and only a dramatic increase in size could justify further developments. In 1863 plans were put forward to drain the common and build houses on it. There was little sympathy for the community which had grown up on the wasteland: 'from living in a house without paying rent, keeping pigs and geese on the Common, and cutting turf without rendering any equivalent, some of the men lead an idle life, and become drunkards or otherwise immoral'. Christ Church, built opposite the lodge to Horton Manor in 1843, had been intended to remedy these defect. The scheme to develop the common was supported by the steward of the manor and the clerk to the board of health; but the board itself was divided. Sir Edward Northey objected to a suburb on the doorstep of his home at Woodcote House, and Thomas Hankey spoke in favour of the open space being left as a lung for London, where parties could come down on the weekend train and picnic among the furze. The interests of London won the day, and the common was preserved. Instead, in 1869, it was the common fields which were enclosed, and development began south and east of the town in Burgh Heath, Worple and College Roads. Off East Street, the houses of the working class were built to fill an area between the two railway lines, sharing space with Young's nursery gardens and Stone's brickyard.

By 1876 Epsom could boast of 'many good and not a few poor houses, spacious and well-filled shops, court-house, market-house, clock-house, water and gas works, banks, a Board of Health, and a weekly newspaper'. There were also two dozen pubs – some, like the *Railway Inn*, purpose-built in the 1850s and others, like the *Barley Mow* and the *Rising Sun*, converted from cottages. Epsom continued to attract wealthy residents; two years later the Clock Tower was covered in flowers and bunting to celebrate the coming of Lord Rosebery and his bride to a country retreat at Durdans. Here the young politician built a noble set of stables, quarrelled with the vicar, and opposed all forms of development. Rosebery Park is a monument to his public generosity and his determination not to let the speculative builders get near Chalk Lane.

Abandoning Chalk Lane, the builders' firms of Longhurst, Furniss, Hopkins and Nye found their opportunity when Epsom Court Farm was divided up for building in 1895. Within 20 years a new landscape of terraced and semi-detached housing had tripled the size of the town. Miles Road alone contained more people than the whole of medieval Epsom.

The progressives of the 19th century could look back with pride. James Andrews, who died in 1915, had been one of the last chairmen of the Board of Health. He had also run the family stationers, printers and bookshop; been Registrar of Births and Deaths and Vaccination Officer; held office as a Schools Manager, and represented Epsom at Queen Victoria's Jubilee. When he spoke to the Literary Institute in 1903, his memories of stagecoaches, candlelight, common fields and cesspools seemed to come from a different world.

Andrews' Board was superseded by an Urban District Council in 1894. It met fortnightly at the Public Hall, situated at the corner of Church Street and Upper High Street. Five years later the council purchased Bromley Hurst, a large house in Church Street, which became an embryo Town Hall until the present building was erected in 1933. Edmund Garrett Wilson, formerly a solicitor in the town, was a clerk to the council for 34 years. He worked many hours a day dealing with major and minor crises and complaints.

Epsom was caught up in the surge of patriotic feeling that came in early August 1914. Local territorial soldiers returning from manoeuvres to Epsom town station were marched to the drill hall, where speeches were made. The soldiers were then quickly entrained once more but this time for active duty. The following month 3,000 volunteers for the University and Public Schools brigade marched into town. Many of them were billeted there for the next ten months. They were quartered for a short time in a hutted camp at Woodcote Park. Later in the war this became a Convalescent Hospital, caring for thousands of soldiers; Horton Manor was also used for the same purpose.

The Downs, so near to the urban area, played a great part in the war effort. From vantage points, special constables scanned the skies for enemy raiders. Training grounds, recruiting camps, rifle ranges and even an explosives factory were dispersed over the broad acres where the sport of kings had once reigned.

On Armistice Day 'the fun – dancing and demonstrating in mad-cap fashion – was maintained till late in the evening. A huge bonfire near the college, consuming an effigy of the Kaiser, frantically excited the youth of the district'. After the war attention returned to the building schemes which were transforming the town.

The London County Council had purchased Horton Manor and its thousand-acre estate as part of a plan for more accommodation and better treatment for the mentally ill. The Manor hospital, partly housed in the old building, was opened in 1899. Horton hospital and St Ebba's, known originally as the Colony, were opened in 1901 followed by Long Grove in 1907. The completion of West Park was delayed by the war until 1924. Altogether, 8,300 patients could be cared for. The five hospitals needed a huge labour force to work efficiently. Doctors, almoners, administrative officers, orderlies, drivers, laundry and kitchen personnel were required; gardeners and labourers were needed to work in the hospital grounds and farms. These London County Council jobs, most of them pensionable, were much sought after.

In the urban area there was development of a more spiritual kind. In 1904 the Congregational church, with seating capacity for 500, was rebuilt. Three years later the foundation stones of the Baptist church (300 seating capacity) were in place. In 1908 the enlargement of St Martin's (up to 1,000 sittings) was consecrated by the Bishop of Winchester. Five years later the Methodist church (capacity for 375) was opened in Ashley Road. Most of the ecclesiastical developments were carried out by local firms, including Cropleys and Longhursts.

The local building schemes of the 1930s were part of the widespread growth of the suburbs around London. The expansion was encouraged by two factors – the electrification of railways, which provided cheap, clean and frequent transport; and the highly-touted opportunity of home ownership for the masses, through long-term mortgages that could be paid off at an affordable weekly rate. Park Lawn Estate was advertised by Wates the builders at 14s. a week for the leasehold. Harwood's Woodcote Green Estate was a superior development (60 years later it is still attractive) and here properties were available at a freehold price of £1,250, fitted with tiled and parquet floors and oak panelling.

There was a rush to build, but not all the building developments were praiseworthy. Less than three miles from the trim flower beds of Rosebery Park, rutted and unmade roads appeared. Unscrupulous speculators had sold plots to individual buyers without providing roads or sewers. The Surrey County Council Act of 1931 and the Ribbon Development Act of 1935 were passed to control building and order the provision of proper services.

In 1934 the Urban District of Epsom expanded to include Ewell. Three years later the Council petitioned for the grant of a charter, which conferred additional power over building developments. By the time that it was granted in September houses were being built in the town at the rate of 1,500 every year.

As early as April 1937, the Council had begun considering air raid precautions. So when war was declared on 3 September 1939, trench shelters had already been excavated, gas masks had been issued and Civil Defence services were ready to be mobilised. Once again Horton became a military hospital. Canadian troops arrived in the area. They were quartered in the grandstand and marched down into the town daily. Over a hundred refugees from the continent were accommodated in large houses until the cessation of hostilities.

Raids by enemy planes came in 1940. Four years later another offensive followed with many attacks by flying bombs. In all, 33 people were killed and 384 injured. But in spite of food rationing, blackout precautions and the effects of six years of war, morale remained high. Towards the end of the conflict enthusiasm for leisure pursuits increased. Epsom Camera Club was formed and the Surrey Philharmonic Orchestra (largely created by local resident Kathleen Riddick) began concerts at the Baths Hall.

The celebratory bonfires of V-Day had spluttered and died but there were still years of austerity ahead. Rationing, which extended to clothes and furniture, continued. On the first day that bread rationing was introduced bakers' roundsmen were four hours late; it was reported that they were clipping coupons and explaining the system to customers.

There was great demand for housing in Epsom, many properties having been destroyed or damaged during the air raids. There were 2,233 applications for housing in council properties. As a temporary measure hutted camps were established, and then pre-fabricated houses – many of them made in America – were erected. It was several years before housing needs were met.

The 1950s saw improvements. The School of Arts and Crafts overflowed from the Technical Institute into converted premises: there were 1,400 part-time students. Large administrative buildings for the Post Office as well as a Civil Defence and

Territorial Army Centre took shape in the East Street area. Epsom District Hospital was enlarged and at Swail House in Ashley Road, 55 flats were built for the blind. It was a time when roads and streets were cleaner, parks and gardens were regularly tended, buses were more frequent and local trains almost always ran on time. However, towards the end of the decade new developers moved into Epsom. They began in a small way, infilling vacant plots in residential areas. Maisonettes were popular – usually four maisonettes to a block and two or three blocks at each location. As time passed, the building firms became more powerful and greedier. Suddenly detached Victorian houses were brought down and three-storey blocks of flats erected. Above the new shops and supermarkets were many floors of office space. Commercial bureaucracy had come to the rescue of the ailing retail trade.

In 1962 Epsom had been 'richer perhaps in late Stuart, Queen Anne and Georgian houses than any other place in Surrey'. During the next two decades, however, a good deal of the richness was lost as buildings listed by the Department of the Environment as 'especially worthy of preservation' were being demolished at an average rate of two a year. Developers demolished large houses – The Shrubbery, Cromwell Lodge, Whitmores and Pitt Place; small houses, shops and weatherboarded cottages; the two remaining cinemas, and Foresters' Hall. Time was rung forever at the *Charter Inn*, the *Railway Hotel*, the *White Hart* and the *Red Lion*. The majority of historic buildings were acquired in good condition, neglected until they became unsafe, and then given demolition consent. Where the council had powers to act, they were not used.

The 1980s brought a different policy towards the continuing expansion of the town. Councillors and planners adopted a more vigilant attitude and local residents became more vociferous, joining conservation groups like the Epsom Protection Society. West Hill House, a council property for many years, was rebuilt in replica after its demolition. The Epsom Church of England Boys School in Hook Road was assimilated into Ben Mhor House, a small office block. The highly successful Laine Theatre Arts School was built to incorporate a small Victorian house.

Concerned about the low level of trade in the 1970s, the council studied proposals for the development of the area round Ashley Avenue – an unoccupied cul-de-sac running parallel with the western end of the High Street. Ten years later the Ashley Centre, a £37 million shopping mall, was being completed. In addition to 40 shops, the centre provided office accommodation, a civic theatre (the Playhouse) and a multi-storey car park for 800 cars.

Recent years have continued the policy of conservation by conversion in Epsom. The municipal baths – looking much the same externally – have been included in a one million pound sports complex and renamed the Rainbow Centre, the *Spread Eagle* has developed a shopping precinct on the southern side and the original well on the common was rebuilt and opened in June 1989.

In 1958 James Chuter Ede wrote about Epsom:

> While living vigorously in the present it has zealously maintained the beauties left to the inhabitants from a historic past, and is laying the foundations for a future in which a full life can be lived in settings in which utility and vision combine to serve our corporate and individual existences.

For ours are Epsom water-drinking wives
And few in that lewd town lead stricter lives.
Thomas Shadwell, Epsom Wells, 1672

Epsom. Its name is known throughout the world. Does not its very mention bring a crowd
of thoughts, ridiculous, sublime, refreshing? Ridiculous when we think of its road scenes on its
racing days; sublime in its recollections, its places; refreshing, when its lovely scenery passes
before memory's eye.
C. J. Swete, Handbook of Epsom, 1860

While there are many disadvantages in living in Epsom – such as lack of public baths,
beautiful parks, handsome structures, and anything in the way of a public library – yet much
may be said in favour of its position on the map.
Touchstone, Epsom Advertiser, 1916

1. Epsom Court had been demoted to a farmhouse when this sketch was drawn in 1830. Originally the demesne farm of the manor, it was leased to tenants after the dissolution of Chertsey Abbey. It was rebuilt in the early 16th century and side wings were added one hundred years later. The farmhouse, whose fields stretched from Longmead to Pound Lane, lay under the present Court Farm Gardens in Manor Green Road.

2. Two hundred years after it was built, the *New Tavern* was occupied by Oldridge the draper (who renamed it Waterloo House) and Bristow's warehouse and forge. Oldridge was succeeded by Wheeler Bros., who acquired the whole building, and later it was acquired by the Elys. The property was first divided in 1820 when the old pleasure grounds were split up into two houses, five cottages, a smithy and a disused cockpit.

3. When this view of the Old Wells was painted in 1796, the surviving corner of its Assembly Room had been converted to a cottage. It still contained 'a piece of old wainscot into which several had cut the initial letters of their names, with the year, purporting, it is supposed, the era some cure was performed'.

4. The Epsom almshouses were built in 1703 on a strip of land donated by John Livingstone the entrepreneur, in Mead Furlong Shot. They stood at 62 East Street and were kept in good repair by the vicar and churchwardens, who had the right to nominate occupants for them. Pulled down in the 1850s, the almshouses were rebuilt in 1871.

5. This picture was sketched in 1812 from the upper windows of the *Spread Eagle*. Every building in the street was subsequently demolished over the next 100 years. The low cottage on the right stood where the post office is now. The overhanging granary was established for a corn chandler, and the building next to it was rebuilt for Thomas Skilton and is now the indoor market. The timber-framed smithy on the left occupied what is now 95 High Street.

News from the Past

6. John Richardson, steward to a Bletchingley gentleman, attended Epsom corn market in 1834 (the year after it was established). Having dined at the *King's Head* and done business at the *Spread Eagle*, he left for home in a gig and was murdered on the lonely road at Buckles Gap. By the time this poster was printed in London, suspects had already been sent for questioning at Epsom.

7. The *Epsom Advocate & Advertiser* ran for three issues only: November and December 1856, and January 1857. The newspaper was printed for Philip Prince of The Hylands in Dorking Road by C. Whiting of the Strand. Prince was also a publisher and author: advertisements for his *Parallel History* and *Monthly Examinations* appeared in his short-lived newspaper.

The Epsom Advocate, AND Advertiser.

No. 1.]   NOVEMBER 1st, 1856.   [ONE PENNY.

WESTON & CO., FOR PIANOS, EPSOM.

The Epsom Observer.

CIRCULATING IN EPSOM, EWELL, ASHTEAD, AND SURROUNDING DISTRICT.

WESTON & CO., FOR ORGANS & HARMONIUMS, EPSOM.

No. 1.   FRIDAY, MAY 10, 1901.   ONE PENNY.

8. Printed in the town by Birch & Whittington, the *Epsom Observer* supported Liberal causes. When Aston, with his Liberal backing, lost the 1906 election it was the end for the *Observer* which two years later merged with the *Advertiser* series of newspapers.

9. The *Epsom & Ewell Times* had become the *Epsom Courier & Ewell Times, Ashtead Kingswood & Banstead Courier* by 1937 and was part of the *Surrey County Courier* series. Howard Browne, a prominent member of the Stoneleigh Residents Association, was the owner of the local newspapers. The last edition was dated 2 September 1939.

10. Crowds being photographed at the declaration of the poll for the 1906 election. William Keswick, the Conservative sitting member, won against Arthur Aston the Radical. Aston had stood seven years earlier as a Conservative, but the mutability of his party convictions did not impress voters.

11. Standing outside the Westminster Bank, three newspapermen of the 1920s survey the Epsom scene. To the left is Rowland (Touchstone) Hedges, reporter for the *Advertiser* for over 30 years, and on the right is James Wall of the *Herald*. Without their indefatigable coverage of local details this book would be much the poorer.

12. This photograph is of Iris and James Wall at their home Tresco in Temple Road, shortly after they married in 1928. James Wall became editor of the *Herald* series of newspapers in 1937 and held the post with distinction until his death in 1945; Iris left her job at the Rural District Council to work with her husband.

13.   These newspaper boys are standing by the horse troughs at the corner of Church Street and the High Street. Behind
the shops at 27 High Street was the newsagents belonging to C. W. Daniell. He stocked magazines, photograph frames and
crested china and, like many local newsagents, published his own postcards.

Faith

14.   The parish church of St Martin, engraved shortly after the 15th-century tower had been reported as being in a ruinous state. Seventeen years later the church was pulled down and rebuilt, all except the tower. Pressure for increased space had already led to the construction of two galleries, one entered by a door in the north wall and the other (for the Lord of the Manor) through an imposing flight of steps at the end of the south aisle.

15.   St Martin's church was rebuilt in 1824 at the instigation of a local committee, which did not include the vicar. William Blomfield of London designed an elegant structure in flint with Bath stone dressings. Large windows were installed which created a light interior and the east window was glazed by George IV's heraldic painter. In the churchyard wooden bedboard memorials, which still survive, can be seen together with the brambles traditionally looped over new gravemounds to deter grazing sheep.

16. When Waldegrave Bainbridge-Bell became vicar of St Martin's in 1904, there was a demand for the rebuilding of the church. In 1907 the Duchess of Albany, widow of Leopold (Queen Victoria's eighth child), visited Epsom to lay the foundation stone. On the left of the picture are Bainbridge-Bell and his wife, with the Duchess of Albany seated, and Mrs. Northey of Woodcote House stand on the right between the Bishop of Winchester and his wife.

17. Lord Rosebery had offered £1,000 to the building fund – on condition that the old structure came down. The new design incorporated features, such as the great tower, which were hardly relevant to the stated aims of the rebuilding fund, established to improve accommodation, ventilation and safety.

18. Bainbridge-Bell's family had thrown their influence into the rebuilding of St Martin's with an eye to his future career. Policy on a Surrey bishopric was still undecided. If Epsom had been able to boast a church of cathedral proportions it might have pipped Guildford to the post as the bishop's seat. Unfortunately by 1924 Bainbridge-Bell had died and the rebuilding of St Martin's church had already been abandoned. The disproportionate chancel and transept (a substitute for the tower) remain incomplete.

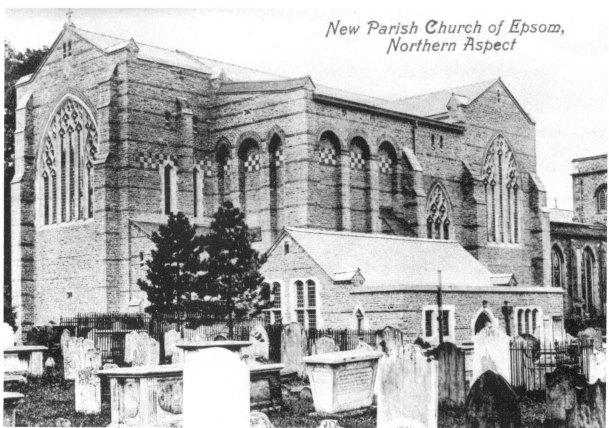

New Parish Church of Epsom, Northern Aspect

19. The organ at St Martin's was constructed in 1909 by Norman and Beard to the designs of Sir George Martin, organist at St Paul's Cathedral. It replaces an instrument installed in 1825, whose organist was hired subject to an agreement that he would only play tunes approved by the vicar and churchwardens, and instruct the children at the National School in psalmody. Subsequent organists, bound by less stringent rules, have included the composer Felton Rapley.

20. Epsom Congregational church, established for non-conforming visitors to the Wells after 1662, suffered from secession in later years. William Bugby bought land in Prospect Place in 1779 and built the chapel, with a house next door for his son the minister. The congregation has now moved to the Salem Baptist chapel in Dorking Road, and the building is a synagogue.

21. John Harris, who began his career at Epsom in 1825 as a Congregationalist minister, preached 'with tender persuasiveness which is calculated to affect hearts which had begun to soften into penitence'. He published 'Mammon', an essay on covetousness in the Church. During his ministry, the Congregational church attracted many of the local gentry, who helped him establish an association for visiting the poor and handing out tracts and books to 300 families.

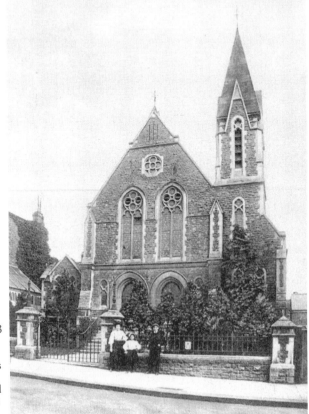

22. The Lecture Hall in Upper High Street was built in 1883 to house the Congregational church's Sunday School. Entertainments put on to hold the dwindling allegiance of children to the Band of Hope included magic lantern lectures (when there was enough gas pressure to light the lantern), violin classes and badminton. John Piper the artist painted backdrops for theatrical performances before leaving Epsom for better things in the 1920s.

23. Christ Church, founded in 1843, was the first Anglican church to be built after St Martin's. The original building was replaced by a larger structure with full parochial rights in 1876. Elizabeth Trotter of Horton Place left the money for this in her will, and the High Church decoration of the interior reflects her family allegiance. Four-fifths of the congregation, however, were working people from the Common.

24. Christ Church vicarage was built in 1876, on the same massive scale as the church, and stood where the present, more modest, house has its lawn. This photograph was taken when the house was occupied by Archer Hunter who arrived in 1881 and remained for 30 years, despite Lord Rosebery's attempts to take him to Mentmore. Hunter superintended the founding of the next Anglican church, St Barnabas, in 1909.

25. Christ Church hall was opened by Rosebery in 1899, replacing a parochial room in West Street. In 1986 it was in its turn replaced by a new two-storey building adjoining the church. The old hall is now used by the Epsom Church Fellowship, a house church founded by Tony and Mary Seton.

26. Horton, like the other mental hospitals, was given a chapel when it opened in 1901. The chapel was divided in the 1960s and half of it is now a hall, named after the Earl of Harewood. It acts as a local Mass centre as well as a place for Anglican worship.

27. The harvest festival of October 1888 at All Saints chapel. The chapel had been built to serve Epsom Union Workhouse off the Dorking Road, near the present hospital. Under the east window, presented eight years before by Lord Rosebery, Frederic Grosvenor the chaplain has hung up a text from the 65th psalm. This was the first harvest thanksgiving held here. After being used for a period as a semi-parochial church, the chapel was demolished in 1967.

28. This children's area was set up in the north aisle of St Martin's and remains in use today. Hugh Warner, vicar from 1938 to 1950, was an active worker for young people and during the War opened a youth centre (the In and Out club) at the old Dorset ironmongers premises.

29. In 1943 Warner also organised the Grasshoppers Club, a weekly get-together at the *King's Head* during which men whose families had been evacuated from the parish could meet for dinner and company. It was part of his campaign to make Christianity relevant to the community.

30. The Open Air Mission workers hoping to save souls at the 1908 Derby. Mission centres were established on local initiative at Woodlands Road and Langley Bottom (afterwards moving into St Stephen's church). In 1893 every public house was visited, with a corresponding drop in trade. Landlords threatened to complain to the Bishop of Winchester.

31.   The officers and committee of the Epsom Brotherhood are seen here assembled at the house of their president, John Beaumont, in 1929. The Brotherhood was established in 1908. Its members, drawn mostly from worshippers at the Congregational church, included Dorset, Chuter Ede, Riddick and Cushine. The First World War had its impact on membership – 178 Brothers served, and 22 died.

32.   Members of the Brotherhood unveil a plaque to John Beaumont. Shortly after coming to Epsom from Purley in 1920, he became President and set about establishing a Provident Club, a Hospital Saving Association, and a magazine (*The Watch Tower*) with a free circulation of five thousand. 'He was a born leader of men and inspired with high ideals of duty and service.'

33. The Ebbisham Hall in
Ashley Road was opened in
October 1929; it was
designed by A. C. Williams
and built by H. H. and
F. Roll. The Brotherhood
raised £18,000 to build this
and the smaller Myers Hall,
partly to house their
organisation and partly as a
public hall; it was licensed
for music, dancing and stage
plays. The halls closed in the
early 1980s, but the façade
has been retained as the
entrance to John Menzies.

Company

34. The *King's Head* was the first inn to be built in Epsom, pictured here c.1830. The adjoining cottage (afterwards separately licensed as the *King's Shades*) seems to have been the original premises, and a larger inn was built beside it on a courtyard plan in the late 17th century. Vestry meetings were held here or at the *Spread Eagle*, and auctions of local property took place.

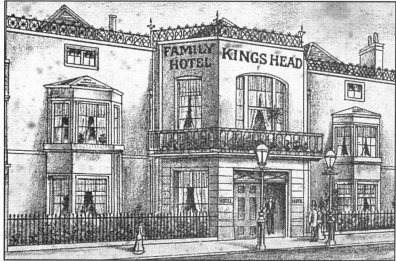

35. By the late 19th century, the appearance of the *King's Head* had been improved by the addition of bay windows and a projecting entrance, which befitted the town hotel. The assembly rooms could seat 120 guests, and the stables beside the bowling green were later joined by motor services. 'The wines, spirits and cigars supplied are of the choicest quality', but this did not soften the hearts of the developers who pulled it down in 1957.

36. In 1903 plans were drawn up by F. G. Burstow of Sutton for alterations to the façade of the *King's Arms* at 118 East Street. It had been a Young's pub since 1880, and the freehold was sold to the brewery in 1908. It is said that beams in the cellar come from men-o'-war that were in the battle of Trafalgar.

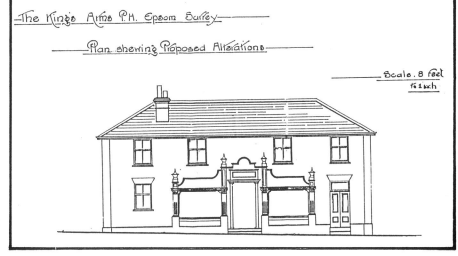

THE QUEEN'S HEAD
EPSOM

37. The *Queen's Head* in South Street was first recorded in 1746. The old building was a weatherboarded cottage, and from about 1800 bore a picture of Queen Charlotte on a unique sign – Her Majesty faced the town centre but turned her back on the road to Dorking. The sign was painted by George Henry Harlow, in imitation of his master Sir Thomas Lawrence. By 1900 the pictorial inn signs in Epsom had been replaced by written ones; the modern picture is a revival.

38. The *Magpie* in South Street was about two hundred years old when it was sketched in 1892. It had passed from John Newans the victualler (1703) through Samuel Wilkinson the brewer (1755) to Hodgsons Brewery of Kingston. In 1943 it became a Courage house.

39. The former coffee house next to the entrance to John Livingstone's New Wells was renamed the *Albion* in 1868. Forty years later it was improved with decorative floral patterns and imitation timber-framing on what had been a sober Georgian façade. This picture of 1939 shows the original windows of the saloon and public bars. Today the bars have been merged into one, and the fittings are reproduction Victorian.

40. A portrait of A. E. Chapman, a popular landlord who ran the *Derby Arms* until 1938. The inn had been owned during the First World War by Walter Langlands, estate agent, auctioneer and member of the Urban District Council. Today the *Derby Arms* is one of the six Charrington houses in Epsom.

41. The Public Hall was designed by J. Hatchard Smith of Downs Avenue (the designer of the *Trocadero Hotel* in London) and opened in 1883. It had separate entrances for the Epsom Club and for the public hall and assembly rooms (licensed for music and dancing in 1907). The Literary and Scientific Society was founded here in 1898, but later outgrew the premises and moved to the nearby Congregational Lecture Hall.

42. The Epsom Common Working Men's Club was founded in 1880 at the expense of James Strange, Lord of the Manor. Funds were later raised by amateur entertainments which sometimes involved the organist and choirboys of Christ Church. By 1910 the 200 members had acquired ownership and management of the club for themselves. Between the wars they organised coach outings for the children of those who lived on the common – a day at Brighton and 5s. each spending money.

43. The Epsom Club split off from the Epsom Town Club in 1914, moving from the Public Hall to The Hollies in Church Street. Its social attractions have ranged from chess to sea-angling The adjoining Conservative Club, founded in 1890, and based in Church Street since 1956, is for those with 'Conservative leanings', whilst the Liberal Club in Upper High Street (founded 1886) makes no political conditions.

Entertainment

44.   A Silver Band has existed in Epsom, under various names, since 1918. The objectives of the Epsom Town Band, its predecessor, were 'to afford its members the means of mental and moral improvement, and rational recreation', fines of 3d. being imposed for smoking in the practice room, attending an engagement with a dirty instrument, and playing whilst drunk.

45.   By the 1950s the band had been renamed the North Downs Silver Band. There are presently 38 members ranging in age from ten to eighty-four. Rehearsals are twice weekly, and the band participates in National and Southern Counties Championships.

46. The hospital at Long Grove had its own theatre in the Recreation Hall, where the staff dramatic society and orchestra played to a reliable audience of patients. It opened in 1907 with Walter Reynolds' play, *Mr. Smith*. English aristocrats, American millionaires, comic Irish servants and the annual pantomime dominated the stage for years to come.

47. Epsom's Little Theatre was founded by Nigel Clarke, an actor and the son of Edward Clarke the landlord of the *Downs Hotel*. In this picture, he appears as the lead in *Ambrose Applejohn's Adventure*. The booking office was at 8 West Street; short seasons ran from 1930 to 1932 at the Ebbisham Hall where actresses such as Peggy Rawlings and Margaret Rutherford appeared.

48. *Rio Rita*, a musical comedy, was staged in January 1936 at the Ebbisham Hall. George Furniss as a Mexican general and Doris Elphick as Marjorie Parker were among local favourites in the large cast. The show was very popular and, as usual, proceeds were given to local charities: the Cottage Hospital was the main beneficiary.

49. The Epsom Operatic and Dramatic Society presented *A Country Girl* in January 1932. The corps de ballet consisted of Mrs. Glenister, Miss Soper, Miss Hart, Miss Fairburn, Miss Rutter, Miss Glenister, Miss Godwin, Miss Childs, Miss Hart and Miss Babbs.

50 & 51. In 1987 Betty Laine built her College for Performing Arts on the corner of East Street and Clayton Road, where the Salvation Army chapel once stood. Students are trained in classical ballet, modern dance and tap, singing, acting and choreography. 'The College demands from its students self-discipline, a sense of responsibility, and a respect of values.'

CINEMA ROYAL

EE! HEAR!   EDWARD HORTON — THE HOTTENTOT   SEE!

52.   Frank Sharp, manager of the Cinema Royal, stands outside with an assistant advertising the new sound system (R.C.A. Photophone) which transmitted the first talkies in Epsom. Sharp ran the cinema for ten years until 1938. During Derby week he booked *The Calendar*, a racing yarn based on an Edgar Wallace novel. Tom Walls' *April the Fifth* won that year, an added boost to local pride.

53. Small properties at 112-118 High Street were replaced in 1937 by the rebuilding of the *George* and the addition of the very modern Odeon Cinema. Well-appointed and large (it seated 1,434 patrons), the cinema survived until 1971. After ten years as an eyesore, the site was developed as a supermarket by Sainsbury's.

54. The Playhouse in Ashley Avenue was opened as part of the site's redevelopment in 1983. Graham Stansfield, the Council's Arts and Entertainments Officer, masterminded the provision of an up-to-date auditorium and backstage facilities. Nicholas Thompson of Penton Howard Wood Levin partnership was the architect. The Playhouse seats four hundred while the adjoining Myers Hall can seat eighty.

On the take board:

TAKE 2	SCENE 157	DATE 1/9/57
LOCATION COACH		TIME 11.55
FILM STOCK PAN F		APERTURE F 3.5
FILM TITLE HOME AND AWAY		WESTON READING 30

55.   A production of 'Home and Away' made by the Epsom Ciné Society in 1957. Geoffrey Walker holds the take board while Cameron Miller and Betty Skipp prepare to act out a dramatic scene. The Ciné Society has adapted to the use of video as well.

56. Hazel Wynn Jones directs while Ann and Geoffrey Walker film on 8mm and 16mm gauge film, respectively. The year was 1958 and a comedy, *Rush-a-bye Baby*, was in production.

57. In the 1690s, raffling had become a popular entertainment for the gentry at the two Assembly Rooms and coffee houses. By the 1860s its popularity had increased throughout the local populace, but reform against drink and gambling were yet to come.

TO BE RAFFLED FOR
AT THE
RAILWAY INN, EPSOM,
On MONDAY EVENING, DECEMBER 16, 1861,
AT EIGHT O'CLOCK,
A HANDSOME GOLD WATCH,
By 130 Members at 1s. each.
The highest throw to claim the Watch; the winner to spend 10s. and the owner the same.

TO BE RAFFLED FOR
AT THE BARLEY MOW, EPSOM,
On MONDAY EVENING, OCTOBER 28th, at 8 o'Clock,
A FAT PIG,
Weighing about 14 stone,
BY 80 MEMBERS AT ONE SHILLING EACH.
The highest throw to claim the Pig, and the lowest to receive 5s.; the winner to spend 5s., and the owner to spend the same.

TO BE RAFFLED FOR
A DOUBLE BARRELLED GUN
With Mahogany Case, complete,
On SATURDAY, SEPTEMBER 21st, 1861,
AT THE MARQUIS OF GRANBY, EPSOM.
TWO SHILLINGS EACH MEMBER.
The Putter-up to spend 8s., and the Winner to spend 8s.

TO BE RAFFLED FOR
AT THE
LOCOMOTIVE, EPSOM,
On Wednesday, February 12th, 1862,
A SILVER WATCH,
By 30 Members at 1s. each.
The winner and putter-up to spend 2s. 6d. each.

58. A panoramic view across the Thames Valley from Epsom Downs in the summer of 1932. 'The finest Downs in the world', Toland wrote in 1711, 'for sheep-walks, riding, hunting, racing, shooting, with games of most sorts for exercise of the body or recreation of the mind, they are nowhere else to be paralleled'. But now the sheep are gone, and the foreground of the view is overgrown with thickets of thorn and briar.

59. Before the coming of the hospitals, Horton Lane was a favourite place for country walks. Only the scattered agricultural buildings (now Horton Park Farm) stood among the fields. By 1907, Lord Rosebery could write to *The Times* about 'the crowds of lunatics met lounging about the lanes of the district in charge of a warder or two'. Ten thousand Epsom people had acquired 5,400 mental patients as their neighbours, and there was bound to be friction.

60. Woodcote Pond was dug to serve the community of the medieval hamlet which grew up along the Upper Green (south of Woodcote Green Road) and Lower Green (west of Chalk Lane). By the 18th century lands taken for Woodcote House had cut the open space in two, and the pond became a play area for the local children. It has recently been relined by K. F. G. Cross of Langley Vale.

61. The waterlogged soil of Epsom Common created a natural playground for children. Families were large and in 1925 Bramble Walk had fifteen neighbouring houses with 45 children between them. Playing in the ponds brought on chest and throat complaints, and illness could close the school for a fortnight at a time: but in summer it was lovely.

62.   After the Great Pond on the common was drained in the 19th century, the area became popular first for steeplechases, then for picnics. In 1912 the Borough Surveyor, Edward Capon, provided work for the unemployed by setting them to clear out the Stew Pond, at 2s. 6d. a day. The pond was used for bathing, and there was a hut where men and boys could pay a penny to change.

63.   The recreation ground off Alexandra Road is the oldest in Epsom. In 1898 the newly formed council bought it after fierce debate in which the expense to ratepayers was justified by recognising the unsuitability of the Downs and Common for organised games, and the need to keep local youth harmlessly occupied.

64.   Part of Court Farm was united with the grounds of West Hill House to form Court Recreation Ground in 1924. Sir Edward Mountain, chairman of the Eagle Star Insurance Co., had left the big house for Norbury Park two years before: and the grounds where guests had danced till late on 3 August 1914 – 'in spite of the heart-stirring war news' – now belonged to the council.

65.   Nelson's swimming pool, next to 30 West Hill, was the official pool for the schoolboys of Kingswood House in the 1950s, although the water came up to their noses even in the shallow end. When it closed in 1964, it was being run by Bill Perkins, ice-cream vendor and keeper of the adjoining pig house. There were rumours that pigs had first refusal of the pool's waters early in the morning.

66. The recreational use of Rosebery Park was confirmed when the Earl gave its eleven acres to the town in 1913. However, rules for its use were strict; games were not to be played and quietude should prevail. However, by the 1930s a bandstand had been erected and on Wednesdays there was music and dancing. At the end of the decade large air-raid shelters were excavated at the southern end of the park.

67. In August 1916 the Military Convalescent Hospital at Woodcote Park was handed over to Canadian forces to be used as a base for their wounded compatriots returning from the Somme. The men pictured here at Rosebery Park were among the 3,000 who recuperated here. To keep them entertained concerts and cinemas were supplemented by the town's first and only baseball league, but the men were still bored and there were outbreaks of violence.

68. Tommy Pearson and Trevor White sitting by a fountain placed through the agency of the Metropolitan Drinking Fountain and Cattle Trough Association, in the summer of 1932. Eleven fountains were built in Epsom's parks and open spaces. The photograph shows one of the earliest fountains, sent to Rosebery Park in 1926, and the only one that remains.

69. Epsom Cycling Club was founded in 1891 – Thomas Hersey the cycle dealer of South Street supplied early racing bikes, including his New Epsom model. When this picture was taken, in about 1935, members would ride to events at Earlswood Common or Crawley, change to racing wheels for the time trials, and return to ordinary wheels for a club run. Nowadays they mostly turn up in cars.

70. Foxes were hunted by the Surrey Union as late as 1912. Meets were held on Tuesdays between Christmas and the end of the season, the hounds being kennelled at Bookham. Stags were turned out for the Surrey Farmers Staghounds at Stamford Pond and were supposed to run north to Ewell; but one at least survived by running into the town and hiding in 52 High Street, Spikesman's china shop.

71. By about 1910 Long Grove Hospital had reached the size of a small town, and like any other small town had its cricket team. Here they are seen posing in front of the pavilion, between Long Grove House and Prospect Villa.

72. Epsom Cricketers Club, established in 1800 by a team of gentlemen, was strong enough to beat Sussex and Middlesex 16 years later. Afterwards the game lapsed and was not revived for some thirty years. Games such as this one on the Woodcote ground were serious affairs; the council cancelled a meeting of the General Purposes Committee for the match on 11 July 1911.

73. Epsom Cricket Club opened their Woodcote ground in 1860, captained by Henry Willis who afterwards played for Surrey. In this 1941 picture they have been playing the Mayor's XI. In the middle of the picture is C. J. Shaw wearing his chain of office, and W. F. Waters is to the right, then Chuter Ede, P. E. Whiteoak Cooper the Town Clerk, and E. E. Schnadhorst who had secured the ground for the club in perpetuity in 1934.

74. Epsom Bowling Club built a new pavilion at their ground in Depot Road in 1914. Bainbridge-Bell (standing centre in the straw hat) made a speech and opened the door of the rustic-looking structure which had cost members a total of £60.

75. In the 1920s the Bowling Club moved to a new ground and new pavilion in Worple Road. In June 1989 they won a last-minute victory over a team from the English Bowling Association.

76. The historian of Epsom College wrote in 1980 that 'All boys, unless excused on medical grounds, are compulsorily exposed to sport'. The games ethic was slow to take root – the first football presented to the school, in 1857, was immediately squashed by an unruly mob – but by 1902, games had become an important part of a schoolmaster's duties.

77. In 1937 members of the Regnal League and their friends were playing impromptu tennis matches on the grass courts and hard courts at Alexandra Recreation Ground. The picture includes; Dennis Roberts, Vera Seymour, Vera Hawkins, Basil Seymour, Heather Pickford, Betty Tucker, Ian Macdonald and Jack Moorcroft.

78. Ebbisham Sports Club succeeded Epsom Badminton Club which existed before the First World War. Originally meetings were held at the Drill Hall in East Street, but when faced with eviction the members formed the Epsom Sports Club Ltd., and found and financed premises in Eastway. The revitalised club was opened by Lord Ebbisham in February 1938.

79. Epsom Golf Club was established in 1889, and quickly gained popularity throughout the county. In the face of hostility from the commoners of Mitcham, Wimbledon and other developing areas, golf enthusiasts looked further afield, and found that Epsom Downs would make a secluded course. The game attracted residents to the middle-class housing south of the town.

80 & 81. By May 1889 the course had been laid and the first competition held. The Club House, completed in 1892, was another Hatchard Smith building. Over a hundred years later the Club still flourishes and now has a ladies and a junior section.

82. Captain's Day, 1984. *Left to right, back row:* A. Richards, R. Page, L. Chenery, T. Goudie, K. Kennedy and M. Smith; *front row:* G. Stannard, D. Young, F. Helder, F. G. Alexander, A. Barnett, P. Roebuck, J. Williamson, A. Hill and K. Edwards.

83. Football began in Epsom with the traditional Shrove Tuesday game, in which two mobs contested the ball up and down the High Street. It continued until 1892 when it was banned as an anarchic sport. The Epsom Thursday team, pictured here at 75 South Street, 1901-2, consisted of local shopkeepers and their sons, who played on Thursday after 4.30 p.m. as this was regarded as early closing time.

84. Epsom Town Football Club was founded in 1917 by a group of young local enthusiasts who gained status in 1924. This photograph was taken after they had created a precedent by winning the league title in their first London League season in 1927, with H. Westlake as captain.

85. Their finest hour came in 1975, when they played Hoddesdon Town in the final of the F.A. Challenge Vase at Wembley. Here the captain Trevor Wales scores Epsom's only goal. Hoddesdon, unfortunately, scored two.

Transport

86. In 1844, as the coaching era came to an end, there were eight up and eight down coaches coming to Epsom or passing through it every weekday. A coach would carry four people on average; two-thirds of them stopped at the *Spread Eagle*. Within a few years the railway had replaced this mode of transport, but coaches appeared again as an Edwardian revival, as seen in this postcard of 1905, and continued on the old Brighton route until the 1930s.

87. In this view, cars, bicycles and horse-drawn vehicles are all crowding the eastern High Street. The people of Epsom were undecided as to whether the traffic jams were a nuisance or preferable to road widening but the Ministry of Transport hoped to speed up the route to the coast and the council agreed with them. Despite a rearguard action by Hatchard Smith (who felt that if people wanted to go fast they should travel by train) street widening was decided on in 1934.

88. Lord Rosebery, seen here riding in a Victoria, kept carriages until his death in 1929. His morning ride was usually in a motor car, but for the evening one he insisted on a carriage, the driver being dressed in the old postillion fashion. Still harassed by insomnia from his stressful political days, he did not return until ten in the evening; people set their clocks by him.

89. The horses that pulled Epsom's carts and carriages required regular watering and cattle troughs were needed by hundreds of animals each day. In 1906 Rosebery commemorated his Derby winner of the previous year by settling a nine-foot trough of grey axed granite outside the Durdans, for the benefit of Chalk Lane traffic. It now stands outside the *Rubbing House*.

90. After the First World War, horse-drawn transport became obsolete except for delivery vans. In this High Street view, motor cars share the road space with two-wheeled traffic. Bicycles had become the working man's transport: the *Wellington* advertised itself as a cyclists' house, and Beauchamp of 6 South Street kept refreshment rooms for them. By 1902, there was a bicycle shed against the dignified walls of Christ Church.

91. The growth of car ownership has begun to cause the familiar sprawl of parked cars in this 1939 view of the market-place. By 1981 there was a car for every three people in the town.

92. In 1913 Woodcote Park House and its estate were purchased by the Royal Automobile Club to provide weekend retreats for its members. The spacious grounds were largely devoted to sports. In this 1974 picture, members of the Austin Seven Club are holding a 'concours d'elegance' and being greeted by A. G. Polson the chairman of the R.A.C. ·

93.   This bus is the 164a, a popular race-course special, seen here arriving at the Downs sometime during the 1920s. The more usual route of the 164 was between Epsom, Banstead, Sutton and Morden.

94.   Buses on the 408 route in 1934, the year after the London passenger transport board came into effect. These covered-top double-deckers became increasingly popular in the 1930s.

95. Derby Day in 1907 showing Epsom Downs station. To the far left of the photograph a London Brighton & South Coast locomotive is bringing Edward VII for a day at the races (Orby won the Derby 100-9). Epsom Downs station still operates, but in a greatly reduced capacity.

96. Tattenham Corner, the second station intended for race goers, was opened in 1901 by the South Eastern Railway. Although approached via Purley rather than Epsom, it was nearer the course, and the 37,000 Derby Day passengers took trade away from the London & South-Western station, which was situated in the town and did not even possess a dining-hall.

97.   The London & South-Western Railway, which had first reached Epsom in 1859, was amalgamated into the Southern Railway in 1923. Two years later electrification took place, and in 1929 the new station was built. Its large entrance hall had a bookstall and tobacconist's kiosk as well as the ticket office. Electric lifts were installed to transfer luggage, mail, fish and parcels from the subway to the platform.

98.   This is the 13.42 Waterloo-Effingham train (c.m.v. 5702) pulling away from Epsom station in 1984. The 60-lever signalbox above the platform, part of the 1919 redevelopment, is no longer in use but survives as a listed building.

SOUTHERN RAILWAY
More Popular Trips for YOU!

WEDNESDAY, JUNE 29		
To Brighton & Hove		
a.m.	From	Fare
11.19	Wallington ...	
11.22	Carshn. Beeches	
11.22	Baustead ...	**4/3**
11.25	Belmont ...	
10.52	St. Helier ...	5/-
10.55	Sutton Comn. .	4/6
10.57	West Sutton ...	
11.25	Sutton	**4/3**
11.28	Cheam	
11.32	Ewell East ...	
11.36	Epsom	4/-

See handbill C.X. 1121

THURSDAY, JUNE 30	From Mitcham J. 11.26 a.m.	From Hackbridge 11.30 a.m.	From Carshalton 11.34 a.m.
To			
PULBOROUGH ...	4/6	4/-	3/6
ARUNDEL ...	5/3	4/9	4/3
LITTLEHAMPTON	5/3	5/-	4/9
BOGNOR REGIS...			

See handbill C.X. 1406

SUNDAY, JULY 3
From Tattenham Corner 10.0 a.m.

To HORSHAM **2/6** ARUNDEL **5/-** PORTSMOUTH & PULBOROUGH **4/-** CHICHESTER **5/-** SOUTHSEA **5/6**

See handbill C.X. 1461

99. Special excursion trains to the coast were advertised locally in 1932. Although they were popular, the pace of travel was slow and excursions had to begin the return journey at an early hour in the evening.

100. The goods yard and sidings off Upper High Street were an important addition to the station of the London Brighton & South Coast Railway which still stands behind nos. 47-57. The station ceased operating in 1929, having become obsolete with the railway merger. Soon after this photograph was taken in 1966, flats were built here.

101. The 1933 model 8 Sunbeam motorcycle (346 cc) was the star of this publicity photograph, taken at Buckles Gap. Barry Bewick of Downside is the rider. The Sunbeams of this era had such a reputation for quality that they were referred to as the gentleman's motorcycle. In 1930, the Sunbeam Motorcycle Club began their annual run to Brighton, which still takes place each March.

Services

102.   The original Cottage Hospital occupied a converted house at Pikes Hill; it had eight beds, and was opened in 1873. The new building in this view was opened in 1889 to commemorate Victoria's Diamond Jubilee. Patients were charged between 5s. and 10s. 6d. a week, but most of the revenue of the hospital came from charity. By 1948, when it passed to the National Health Service, there were 40 beds.

103.   The mental hospital at Horton was built in 1901, to the same design as that at Bexley, and similar layouts were later used at Long Grove and West Park. The overpowering effect of a central block of wards was softened by the provision of outlying villas and the landscaping of the grounds, kept trim by over a hundred patients.

104. Great efforts were made to turn the mental hospitals into self-sufficient communities. Soon after it opened, Long Grove had a tailor's shop turning out 1,100 pairs of trousers annually, a shoemaker's repairing 2,000 pairs of boots, and an upholsterer's manufacturing 940 brooms and brushes. These workshops were intended to be therapeutic as well as commercial, and at least half the patients had some kind of employment.

105. Staff at the mental hospitals, like these kitchen workers at St Ebba's (then the Epileptic Colony) had to organise the catering on a grand scale. In 1909 the residents of Long Grove were consuming 100 tons of meat, brewing up 15,000 pounds of tea, and smoking 3,000 pounds of tobacco in 400 dozen clay pipes. Much of the food came from the farms, now part of the Horton Country Park.

106. Swail House was the first set of flats to be custom-built for the blind when it was developed in the Victorian grounds of Worple House, Ashley Road, in 1952. The London Association for the Blind (now Action for Blind People) named the property after Martha Swail of Hammersmith, with whose legacy it was bought. It provides 55 flats where blind people can lead independent lives.

107. Mittendorf House at 18 East Street was named after another benefactor and formed the Epsom home of Dr. Barnardo's. A hundred Barnardo's boys used to attend Pound Lane School in a uniform of polo-neck sweaters and shorts. The home was closed during the war when the boys were evacuated. In 1956 the post office was built on the site.

108. The council school at the corner of Pound Lane and Hook Road was built to accommodate a thousand children. 'Education revolved around lots and lots of lists – lists of kings and queens, lists of countries and lists of the capitals of those countries, lists of rivers, oceans and mountain ranges; but above all there were lists of dates. Everything there was seemed to have a date either of when it was born, died, discovered, founded, invented or lost'. Pound Lane School was built in 1907.

109. The school had a tradition of putting on a concert at the end of the summer term, with fancy dress and maypole dancing. This photograph was taken home in 1913 by D. H. Tugwell, aged six.

110. John Propert, a Welsh surgeon, established a Medical Benevolent College in 1853 on land given by Dr. Graham of Epsom. By 1882, when the house system was introduced, Epsom College had been brought into line with other public schools on matters such as hygiene, discipline, and a low teacher-pupil ratio. Parents were assured that the schoolboys were kept in seclusion throughout Derby week.

111. 'No finer body of young men is sent out into the world by any school than is sent out by Epsom College', said Rosebery at the Jubilee in 1905. Gymnastics was the most important sport in the 1890s, providing three public schools champions; it was part of the process by which the school 'turns out Englishmen and English gentlemen healthy in mind and body, ready to go anywhere and do anything'.

112. In 1915 many ex-public schoolboys, anxious to play a part in the First World War, were being housed in barracks on the Woodcote Park estate. The War Office, which had commandeered the land, contracted Humphreys of Knightsbridge to build huts, a chapel, and a recreation room.

113. In June the barracks were taken over as a convalescent hospital for Australian and New Zealand soldiers returning from Gallipoli and the Somme. Over 4,000 men needed something to occupy their time and the concerts and moving pictures at the recreation hall were supplemented by billiards, boxing, shooting and skittles.

114. The ornamental garden of the Ashley Road police station is the setting for this photograph showing members of the Epsom force in 1912. The garden was soon to be the scene of violence after two Canadian soldiers from the Woodcote Park Convalescent Camp got into trouble at the *Rifleman* in 1919. They were locked in the cells, but their companions rioted and attacked the station with broken fencing and stones from the rockery. Sergeant Green (third from left in the second row) was killed.

115.   Epsom Fire Brigade in its horse-drawn days. In 1869, after Chadband the tailors had burnt down while volunteer forces dug for the hydrant and waited for the hose to turn up, a brigade was appointed under Mr. Busbridge as superintendent and James Furniss as foreman. The engine and part of the hose was kept under the Clock Tower, with the rest of the hose kept in East Street and at West Hill – which must have presented some problems of organisation.

116. The present Fire Station in Church Street was built in 1937 to replace a smaller station which had been on the site since 1911. It cost £21,000 and the design by Pite Son & Fairweather was a 'nice modern front' in the magisterial judgement of Pevsner. Two fire appliances and two motor ambulances were housed here and flats were provided for the firemen.

117. Post Office workers stand in front of their headquarters in 1907. The building was built nine years earlier in the early Tudor style. Inside, 18 tills were installed to cope with the pressure of work anticipated during Derby week. Meanwhile the 26 postmen walked with deliveries as far as Ewell and Walton-on-the-Hill. The two men with sashes have received them for long service.

118.   Nora Willis, seen here under instruction in 1915, was the first woman to be formally employed by the Post Office. Shortly afterwards Frances Hamilton Pott joined her, and their joint labours relieved a postman for service at the front. Cinematograph newsreel companies, attracted by the phenomenon of women working, petitioned Epsom's postmaster but to no avail: war or no war, Miss Willis was not to appear in the newsreels.

119.   The non-conformist chapel at Epsom Cemetery (now demolished) was designed by William Young in 1870, together with its Anglican twin and the lodge and gates. By 1923 space was running out, and the Council approached Rosebery for more land; but he was still smarting over their condoning football in Rosebery Park, and charged £2,000 for his field – giving the money to charity.

120. The Treasurer's department of the Town Hall was mechanised after the War. Pauline Childs, on the right of the picture, is working the punch card operator, a Power Samas machine which encoded details of names and addresses, while Audrey Goff, on the left, is on the printer which produced rate demands, invoices and wage slips. In the centre Ann Connolly superintends a machine for revising codes as values changed.

121. These two dustcarts at the council works in Depot Road illustrate 20 years of progress. The 1937 model on the left was a simple side-loader; the 1958 machine on the right loaded at the back and compressed rubbish automatically – 18,000 tons being disposed of each year. Both were replaced by a wheelie-bin system in 1990. Dustmen give more satisfaction (93 per cent) than any other council service.

122. In this 1953 view of the pumping station at East Street the plant is extracting water from two wells, a borehole and 280 ft. of adits in the underlying chalk – 36 gallons a day for each inhabitant of the town. The first well was sunk a century before, and water was pumped directly into the mains or reservoirs; since 1938 it has been sterilised.

123. In 1896 the Epsom Technical College, a centre for study classes, was opened in Church Street. The building was a Hatchard Smith design and stood on land given by Basil Braithwaite of Hookfield. Rosebery, in his opening speech, saw the institute as a means by which 'a man might fit himself to be a skilled artisan in his trade'. Under its first principal, W. H. Osmond, the Institute offered lessons in carpentry, shorthand, cookery and French.

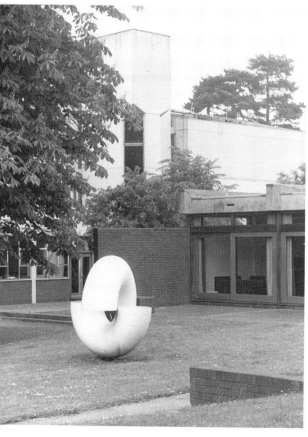

124. Later the emphasis shifted to art: Frederick Spencer Gore, the British artist from South Street, gave lessons and from 1930 to 1961 David Birch R.A. was principal. In 1973 new premises in Ashley Road were designed by the County architect R. J. Ash to house the Epsom School of Art and Design, which now offers courses in fine art and fashion, three-dimensional and communication design.

Business

125 & 126. Camellias, azaleas, fuchsias and roses were flourishing in the nursery which George Dods acquired from Charles Young in 1860. Where the waterworks and Rainbow Centre now stand were a propagating house for geraniums and a New Holland house to nurture Australian and South African imports. Frank Giles took over the adjoining firm of Morse Bros. in 1934; he is seated in the centre of his staff in the photograph below.

127. Robert Dearle, tallow chandler and oilman, occupied premises at 100 High Street (now the entrance to Sainsbury's) which had been acquired by his father before 1797. Soap and candles were made from tallow in a workshop at the back – 'on candle making days the whole street reeked of fat', and the council paid special attention to the area when they fumigated the street after Derby week. Dearle died in 1906, having attended eighty successive Derbys without ever betting on one of them.

128. William Barnard's family business was already 50 years old when he came to Epsom in 1855. He set up shop at 115 High Street, offering 'Ball & Route Suppers and Wedding Breakfasts supplied on the shortest notice'. His successor, G. Riddington, had converted the shop to a tea-room by 1911 and retailed from the pastrycook's next door.

129. Charles Churchill was left £200 by his father to set up as a saddler at 30 High Street (in front of the present Woolworth's); there was another shop at Ewell. He sold everything from carriage lamps to stable brooms, but specialised in making race and hunting saddlery. Shoppers were accustomed to hearing gun-shots from the back of the shop, as he also traded as a horse-slaughterer.

130 & 131. Ernest George Pullinger began working for James Andrews the stationer and printer in 1888. He purchased the business in 1915, later becoming the town Registrar and an insurance agent. After Pullinger's had moved to 56 High Street in 1937, his sons Frank and Phillip ran the firm. Frank's son Nicholas was in charge when the business closed at these premises in 1992.

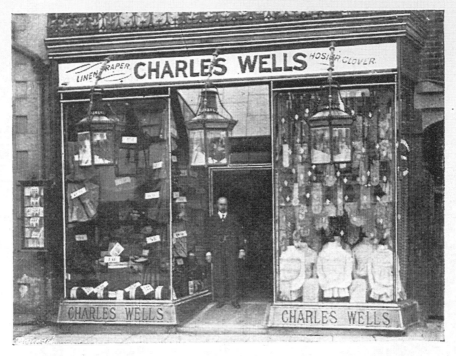

Telephone P.O. 263.

Linen Draper & Silk Mercer, Hosier and Glover.

Show Room for MILLINERY, MANTLES and JACKETS.

Each department contains the latest
:: and most up-to-date Novelties. ::

QUALITY the very best. DRESSMAKING a Speciality.

Best Workmanship. Finest Materials.

Charles Wells,

Note the Addresses—

High Street and Brighton House,
— EPSOM. —

Ladies & Children's Outfitting & Baby Linen at Brighton House.

132. Charles Wells, who has recorded himself for posterity in this advertisement, sent in plans for an elaborate shop to be called Brighton House in 1903. With the forbiddingly high rental of £206 a year, the property and business was taken over by Nelson Ayles in 1915.

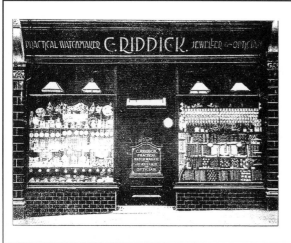

133. Charles Riddick lived above the jeweller's shop which he rented at 27 Upper High Street. His daughter went on to achieve fame as a conductor and the founder of the Surrey Philharmonic, and made several broadcasts (*see* illustration 168).

134. Aberdeen House at 2 West Street continued as a butcher's until the 1980s. The shop still retains a splendid glass-panelled cashier's desk. Ardern Elphick (1840-1927), who followed George Bradnam and was succeeded by Matthews at these premises, has allowed his advertisement to give a false impression of his age: the same photograph was used repeatedly for twenty years.

135. Sebastian Lang (1898-1967) opened his high-class establishment in the late 1920s. Permanent waving was a long elaborate process, so Lang's salon remained open until late in the evening. With the addition of gentlemen's hairdressing the business continued until the 1960s.

136. Thomas Skilton, landlord of the *Leg of Mutton & Cauliflower* in Ashtead, also owned a dairy farm that supplied milk to Epsom College from 1853 onwards. By 1892, Henry Skilton had established a base in Epsom at 107 High Street. His cows were kept at Court Farm, where green fields still backed onto the new developments around Hook Road.

YOUR DAIRY!

PHONE : 866

THE DAIRY *of* HIGH ENDEAVOURS!

Licensed for "Certified" Milk

All Milk direct from Farms

BEST SUPPLIES AND HOME AND EMPIRE PRODUCE ONLY

Not in any way connected with Combines or Trusts

137. 17 Church Street, originally a small printing shop for Birch and Whittington, became a dairy in 1926. The dairy continued until the mid-1950s: the property is now a betting shop.

138 & 139. The printing firm established by William Dorling in 1821 was brought into the 20th century by his grandson, Henry Mayson Dorling. His official position as Clerk of the Course was supplemented by an unofficial title as Dictator of Epsom; 'everybody hates me', he said, 'and I love it'. Race cards for the Derby were first printed on an Albion press seen here at the works in Depot Road.

140. In 1824 James Chandler left the ironmongery trade to set up as a rival to Pagden's brewery at Church Street. His successor on the South Street site, William Bradley, built this brewery for ale and porter in the 1870s but closed 30 years later: Pagden's survived to see their centenary. Bradley pubs (the *Ladas* and the *Wellington*) have now passed to Charrington, and Pagden ones (including the *Amato*) to Friary Meux.

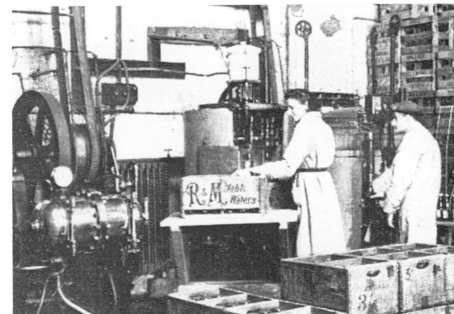

141 & 142. The premises at 18 South Street where George Randall set up his soft drinks firm passed out of the family on his death in 1912 but were reacquired by his son Percy, who had returned from travel in New Zealand with an improved knowledge of the trade. He established a new factory at the rear of 55 South Street in 1935, making ginger beer, real fruit squashes and carbonated drinks.

143.   The first trains ran from Ewell West to Epsom in 1859. Stone and Swallow, the brickmakers of London Road in Ewell, took the opportunity of opening fresh works off East Street from which goods could be loaded directly onto the railway sidings. From this site (now the Kiln Lane Trading estate) came the bricks, tiles, drainpipes and garden pottery which the firm manufactured until it closed in 1938.

144.   There were several factories on the industrial estate, now redeveloped, to the south of Ashley Avenue. In this one, on the site of Bradley's brewery, engineering parts are being made for the war effort in 1943. R. Webb, second from the right, is making wing parts to connect the fuselage of an aircraft. He had moved with the firm from Oakhill Road in Sutton, his wages being increased from 10½d. to 1s. 1d. per hour in consequence.

145 & 146. Epsom builders were kept busy on this High Street site. The view on the upper left shows the premises built for Lucy Andrews' printing and stationery firm being pulled down in 1931, in advance of road-widening. Lloyds Bank, understanding that the scheme had fallen through, built a new bank on the same site, only to have it demolished by the council when the road-widening was resumed two years later. The present bank, finished by 1937, stands about ten yards behind the old one.

147. Freddie Plume, carpenter and joiner, was one of the finest stairmakers in Surrey. In the early 1920s he was employed by Charles Norrington (builder), whose office and works at 44 Upper High Street continued in trade until 1972. Timber came from Longhurst's yard beside the railway.

148 & 149.   Workers for Howard & Co. of Covent Garden rebuilt the Grandstand. They began in the week after the 1926 Derby and completed (providing accommodation for 20,000 racegoers) on the night before the 1927 Derby. Work would have been easier if the General Strike had not cut off supplies of girders; short ones had to be riveted together to run the 700-ft. length of the building. Afterwards there was a completion dinner given by the Earl of Lonsdale.

150. These are the stables at Priam Lodge, Burgh Heath Road, in 1896. Nearby, on the edge of the Downs, were the South Hatch (Nightingall), Shifnall (Ellam) and Mospey (Whitburn) establishments. Less than a mile away, the Wootton family who owned Treadwell House in Downs Road had stables containing 30 stalls.

151. William Bristow ran livery stables beside the *Spread Eagle* and owned the Pantechnicon warehouse and shoeing forge at Waterloo House. His son Harold (Fred) Bristow (1906-65) is shown here at Longhurst's the undertakers, where he worked for over 30 years, sometimes driving their vehicles. His son John Alastair Bristow began his motor accessory business in 1959 and now has a fleet of Rolls-Royces for hire.

152. The wheelwright's business at the corner of Dorking and Woodcote Roads, established by Thomas Field in 1852, expanded its business to include motor works and today, by a gradual evolution, has become a B.P. service station.

153. More ambitious designs were to follow. This view of 1935 shows the Woodcote Motor Co. garage in Church Street. It had replaced the Old Lodge and its extensive gardens, and was built in the Art-Deco style. The Company were agents for Austin and Rover, distributors for Buick, Hillman, Humber, Morris, Triumph and Wolseley. The property passed first to University Motors and then to H. F. Edwards.

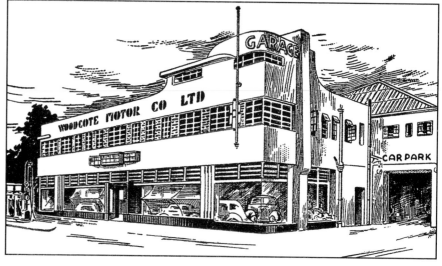

154. The Electricity Showrooms in Church Street (now Seeboard) were designed in 1937 by Williams, Pettett & Gardner of Ashley Road. In the demonstration and interview rooms, ratepayers were persuaded to buy or hire 'all kinds of domestic electrical apparatus, including cookers, water heaters, washboilers, kettles, cleaners and refrigerators etc.'. Between 1920 and the outbreak of war, electricity consumption in the town went up by 20 per cent each year.

155. Elizabeth Evelyn, the Lady of the Manor, was granted the right to take profits from a market and two fairs in 1685. The fairs were never popular, and the market had to be renewed in 1833. At the beginning of this century, when the grant lapsed again, Thomas Hersey revived it by erecting stalls outside Waterloo House and defying the council to remove them. The council, which has since succeeded Mrs. Evelyn as Lord of the Manor, is now anxious to promote the market.

156. In 1840 a shop on the corner of Waterloo Road and the High Street was taken over by Robert and Andrew Burn, ironmongers. By 1887 they had sold out to William Dorset, who ten years later sold the right-hand half of the premises to the London and County Bank and rebuilt the remains of his own shop in Tudor style, with a plough on the roof by way of advertisement. Dorset specialised in agricultural and gardening stock, plumbing and kitchen ranges.

People

157. James Chuter Ede (1882-1965), Epsom's Charter Mayor, was born over the grocer's shop owned by his father James Ede, and rose to be Home Secretary in the post-war Labour government. His uncle supported him at Cambridge, and on returning from war service in the East Surreys he stood unsuccessfully as Labour candidate for Epsom in 1918. Later, he was elected first for Mitcham and then for South Shields. His long career in politics included shaping the Education Act of 1944. His brother Noel, who was committed to the Communist Party, had a less distinguished career; his rallies at the Clock Tower were broken up by police.

158. Thomas Miles (1827-99), *above left*, ran the greengrocery shop at 143 High Street and worked as a market gardener. He would 'unhesitatingly inform carriage folk that they could have the strawberries (or other fruit) when they were picked and nothing would move him to speed up the process'. Miles Road, which was built on his field, is named after him.

159. Tom White (1853-1902), *above right*, was a popular racing correspondent; his nom-de-plume was Sunrise. He lived at Vine Cottage, a detached villa in Clayton Road. He was killed in an accident when driving his gig back from Kempton Park Races – fully three hundred people attended the funeral. At a benefit matinée held at the Royal Music Hall in Holborn, a thousand pounds was raised for his widow and eight children.

160. Herbert William Cushine (1899-1963)– 'Bill' Cushine was one of the first pupils at the Pound Lane School in 1907. He joined a shipping company and travelled the world at an early age; after service with the Royal Field Artillery 1915-19, he joined a city printing firm. His contributions to the council included arranging the purchase of Court Recreation Ground, and opening the municipal baths in 1939, the year he was Mayor.

161. Happy Jack (fl.1910) was a colourful character who appears in caricatures and photographs of the time. He lived – as far as anyone knew – on the Common, was fond of drink and appeared regularly before the local magistrates.

"HAPPY JACK"

162. Thomas Hersey (1855-1932), shown here in the shop doorway, spent most of his industrious life in Epsom. Apprenticeship in the coaching trade led to his own business in motorcyles and then motorcars. Hersey battled for good causes. He defended rights of way over the Common against actions by the railways; he fought moves to keep gypsies and motorists off the Downs. His seven properties in South Street were aptly named Controversy Cottages.

163 & 164. Lester Bowden (1906-80) took over the tailoring establishment founded at 10 Upper High Street by his father Arthur, and three years later in 1930 moved to the present premises, 109-113 High Street. Bespoke tailoring was augmented with the supply of riding clothes to trainers and jockeys nationally. Later Lester's sons Warwick and Richard took over the business reins. By 1991 they were able to open a new venture, a superstore at Hatfield.

The Shop in EPSOM for quality and service (unique these days). School outfitters to many local schools including ROSEBERY. In your own interest please order Summer Uniform as early as possible.

Lester Bowden

HIGH STREET
(opposite Post Office)
EPSOM

165.   This 1920s caricature shows George Two-Hats Southon, who wore a pair for safety in his tree-felling trade – Edward Capon, Borough Surveyor and champion of Fire Brigade efficiency – George Duller a colourful jockey – Lord Rosebery out for carriage exercise – Stanley Wootton the dapper local trainer – and M. H. Benson, the bookmaker who owned The Grove and later Highfield in Burgh Heath Road.

166.   Edward James Clarke, when not supporting cross-country running, was for many years the landlord of the *Downs Hotel* (now the *Rubbing House*). The Hotel was very close to the winning post by the grandstand and to attract and facilitate the work of newspapermen and bookies telegraph and telephone links were installed.

SURREY CROSS-COUNTRY CHAMPIONSHIP.—By Frank Lazenby.

There was a big entry for the seven miles Championship at Epsom.

167. Alfred Charles Marshall (1886-1958) became manager of the family fish business in 1924. Seven years later he was founder-president of the National Federation of Retail Fishmongers and Poulterers. His interest in local affairs peaked in 1942 when he became Mayor. After his death, his sons Hector and Norris looked after the family shops and restaurants until 1981.

168. Kathleen Riddick stands to the right of her father Charles, dressed in cockney costume for a fancy dress party in this 1925 photograph. She went on to achieve fame as a conductor and founder of the Surrey Philharmonic, and made many broadcasts.

169 & 170. John Parkhurst used his linguistic gifts for 'the cause of Christian faith and moral virtue', publishing first a grammar and lexicon of the Hebrew language (1762) and then another for Greek (1769). These works were reprinted several times for those who wished to read scripture in the original. In 1754, on his marriage to Susanna Myster of the Cedars, Parkhurst moved to 24 Church Street where he died in 1797.

171 & 172. In 1785 Parkhurst was able to settle a fellow enthusiast for phililogy, Jonathan Boucher, as vicar of Epsom. It was ten years since Boucher, an American loyalist, had left Maryland as an exile. He and his library of ten thousand books moved into the Old Vicarage, then to Woodcote House (shown here before the Regency façade was built) and then in 1789 to West Hill, where he wrote his *View of the Causes and Consequences of the American Revolution.*

173 & 174.   The author of Mrs. Beeton's cookery book was born Isabella Mayson. She was seven years old in 1843 when her widowed mother moved to Epsom to marry Henry Dorling. For the next 13 years she lived at Ormonde House, a large property at the eastern end of the High Street which had to accommodate the large Dorling family, lending library and printing business. It was not until after Isabella had left Epsom, on her marriage to Sam Beeton in 1856, that she achieved fame with her *Book of Household Management*.

175.   In 1845 Mary Moffat married David Livingstone, then a visitor to her South African home. He was not very flattering about her – 'a stout stumpy body' – but thought that a missionary needed a wife. Seven years later, thinking that their children needed proper education, Livingstone sent Mary to England with them. The Directors of the London Missionary Society found lodgings for her in Epsom, and paid for her children's education at the Eisdell's school in The Cedars.

176 & 177.   Archibald Primrose, 5th Earl of Rosebery, bought the Durdans in 1874. From here he planned a programme of horse-breeding that led to the Derby victories of Ladas in 1894 – celebrated in the engraving – Sir Visto in 1895 and Cicero in 1905. At the same time he rose in the Liberal party, attending to Scottish issues; in 1886 he was Gladstone's Home Secretary, and eight years later succeeded him as Prime Minister. Rosebery's government fell the next year, and he retreated from political reponsibility into local government.

178 & 179. Arthur Nightingall received his greatest acclaim for riding the winner of the Grand National on three occasions. In this 1896 photograph he is shown, aged 28, against the door of Priam Lodge in Burgh Heath Road. The Nightingall family were associated with racing and Epsom until the 1960s, but Priam Lodge passed into other hands – Pendarves, Greentree, Kindersley, Butcher and other trainers. In 1991 the building was converted into self-contained flats.

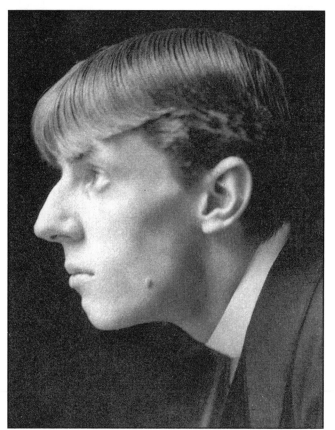

180 & 181. In 1881 Aubrey Beardsley, aged nine, was circulating little sketches of flowers and children from his home at 37 Ashley Road. Fifteen years later, knowing that he was dying of tuberculosis, he returned to Epsom and stayed in two rooms at the *Spread Eagle*. Here, working by candlelight before windows obscured with black curtains, he perfected the classical obscenity of the Lysistrata drawings.

182 & 183.   John Piper left Epsom College in 1921 after winning the drawing prize, and went on to study at the Royal College of Art and the Slade. He worked as a war artist and afterwards abandoned his earlier interest in the abstract for a style of romantic landscape painting, with the emphasis on buildings. This view of his family home at 47 Ashley Road was drawn for J. M. Richards' *The Castles On the Ground*.

184.   Jimmy Page, below left, grew up in a semi-detached house in Miles Road. His first ambitions were as an artist, and he attended Sutton Art School, but on joining the Yardbirds to play guitar he reformed the group in partnership with Robert Plant from West Bromwich. In 1968 the group played its first gig as Led Zeppelin at Surrey University, and within a few years Page had moved on from performing folk masses for St Barnabas to an unprecedented world-wide sale of rock albums. Led Zeppelin split up in 1980.

185.   Below right can be seen the artists for the newly formed 'Eagle' comic who moved to Epsom in 1950, and soon afterwards found studio space in 1a College Avenue. Frank Hampson (on the right of the photograph) set the pace with the exacting standards of his Dan Dare strip; beside him are Don Harley and Robert 'Pop' Hampson. All the Treens, Phants and Pescods of the drawn strip were based on carefully posed photographs such as this one, and passers-by got used to seeing artists blaze away with space-guns in College Avenue. Hampson left the 'Eagle' in 1961.

Racing

186. When pony racing formed part of the Coronation celebrations in 1953, 'The Tout' seized the opportunity to caricature some Epsom trainers – such as Tommy Gosling, Jack Dines, George Edward Fuller, Vic Smyth, Stanley Wootton and Staff Ingham. Famous jockeys included Gordon Richards, Charlie Smirke and Ken Gethin.

187. The Derby course is a mile and half long – climbing at first, then after a level turn descending at Tattenham Corner, and ending in a rise before the winning post. 1927 brought the BBC to the Downs for their first outside broadcast of the race, and this 'Radio Times' drawing by Eric Fraser has all the necessary details. The Derby was first televised in 1931.

188. The main pedestrian route to the Derby was up Chalk Lane, but no attempt at traffic control was made until the arrival of the motorcar. Lovers of the turf could obtain permission to go through Rosebery's grounds at Worlds End, passing the graves of the four locally trained winners. Victoria and Albert, on their only visit in 1840, had a special road made through Woodcote Park to the Paddock, courtesy of Baron de Teissier.

189. The attractions of the fair, switch-backs and merry-go-rounds, have competed over the years with more topical entertainments – Barnum's freaks at the turn of the century, Sir Malcolm Campbell's Blue Bird in 1933. Tipsters and touts have shared space with magicians and nigger minstrels, and fortune-tellers have offered predictions about life or horses. The Dip Fair was held in the crook of Tattenham Corner until 1971, when it moved south of the course.

190. At five in the morning on the day of the race, visitors would queue for a wash and brush-up at these horse troughs on the corner of East Street and the High Street. The Council supplied soap and towels for early risers – gypsies, the first racegoers, and Dorlings staff about to load the racecards at the Upper High Street station.

191. The size of the Derby crowd is hard to measure. Until recently it was estimated at half a million. Before any public transport was available, it was 128,000; in the 1870s, after Epsom Downs station was opened, perhaps double that figure; and double that again when the new grandstand was built to take increased numbers in 1927. Since then there has been little increase. In the background of this view is the old grandstand, built in 1830 and leased to Henry Dorling fifteen years later.

192. In this view from the back, the 1830 Grandstand (from which the flag is flying) has been overtaken by Victorian accretions. In the foreground is the Prince's stand, named after George IV but rebuilt in 1879 after a fire. To the left is the Great War building, built in 1914 for stableboys and staff but almost immediately requisitioned as a war hospital.

193. This is the 1927 Derby, when the new Grandstand was opened and Frank Curzon's Call Boy was the Derby winner. Visitors – including the royal family and Captain Lindbergh of the first transatlantic flight – were occupying the largest race-stand in the world. It accommodated 20,000 people, whilst its predecessor had only housed six thousand. In 1991 the left-hand side of the grandstand was replaced by a new building, the first to accommodate other leisure activities as well as racing.

194. From the earliest days, the Derby crowd has been a curious blend of the ruling and working classes . Even the topography of the Downs was an image of equality – 'the poorest creature on the course can see the sight, with a little pushing and squeezing, as well as the Princes and Princesses'. The crowd in this 1872 engraving has rushed onto the course after a race, a practice which continued until 1918. A tunnel under the course, made to protect the precious turf from wear, was built in 1963.

195. 'Weaving all around, between the picnics, the carriages, the tents and sideshops, were the wandering pedlars and entertainers: acrobats and stilt-walkers, gypsy fiddlers and nigger minstrels, palmists and flower-sellers.' These 1860s acrobats have set up camp for the week. About this time Show Out Sunday (the fair held the Sunday before the Derby) was introduced.

196. About a thousand gypsy families – perhaps a quarter of Britain's Romany population – turn up each year for Derby week. In 1937 the Epsom Downs Conservators intensified a policy of removing caravans, and Lady Sybil Grant stepped in as the gypsies' protector. Here Lena Cooper stands in the field on the Durdans estate where she stayed after being evicted from the Downs; she is holding her baby, born during race week 1937.

197. Police at the Derby today are usually less obtrusive than this 1923 turnout. The crimes which preoccupied the Victorians – prostitution, suicide, bare-fist fighting – gradually dwindled, though thimble-rigging (a simple conjuring trick to cheat gamblers) continued for a century after Frith illustrated it in his great panorama (1860). The magistrates' court under the old grandstand, where summary justice was dealt out to offenders on the course, has not been retained.

198.   Afterwards 'through the white dust, and the drought of the warm roads, the brakes and carriages and every crazy vehicle rolled towards London: orange sellers, tracts sellers, thieves, vagrants and gypsies made for their various quarters – roadside inns, outhouses, hayricks, hedges or the railway station. Down the long hill the vast crowd made its way, humble pedestrians and carriage folk. At the *Spread Eagle* there would be stoppage for a parting drink.'

199.   The 1896 Derby was a patriotic spectacle. Persimmon, the winner, had been bred at Sandringham by the Prince of Wales and the crowd went wild as his jockey, Jack Watts, forced him ahead of Rothschild's St Frusquin in the last hundred yards. Hats were thrown in the air and the cheers went on for fifteen minutes as Edward led in his horse. The 'Prince's Derby' was the first to be filmed as a popular newsreel.

Loyalties

200. This bonfire was built on the Downs for Victoria's 1897 Jubilee. The Council had draped the Clock Tower and lamp-posts with flags and coloured muslins, there were glow-lamps in front of the *Spread Eagle* and a portrait of the Queen 'Loved By All' hung over the *King's Head*. Schoolchildren were marched off to a special playground behind the regimental band of the East Surreys. Parents watched competitors climb the greasy pole for a leg of mutton.

201. For the coronation of 1902, Walter Langlands brought a Devon ox and had it slaughtered by Polhill & Sons at 19 High Street. Council workmen, including Mr. Skinner (front of photograph) were given the task of roasting it, and the flesh of this remarkable animal was sufficient to feed 1,200 people in the adjoining marquee.

202. Sir Edward and Lady Northey posed for this photograph on their return to Woodcote House after attending the 1937 coronation. Meanwhile a general committee of 141 people had organised the united religious service, the distribution of commemorative beakers to children, the fancy dress and a torchlight procession. The Grandstand lent tableware for the old people's luncheon, the Electricity Showroom supplied electricity free of charge for the illuminations and the official souvenir programme was designed by the School of Art.

203. On Saturday 12 June 1953, three days after her coronation, Elizabeth II made a private visit to the Derby. Leaving the Downs by a different route, the royal party did not see the elaborate decorations that had been put up in the High Street. The Fire Brigade fixed the crown at the *Spread Eagle* crossroads, the Chamber of Commerce paid for bunting on minor roads, and David Birch R.A. approved the colour scheme. 'Nowhere did I find so much effort had been made to make a festive scene as at Epsom', wrote a 'staunch Royalist' from Woodcote Green.

204. In June 1977, the year of her Silver Jubilee, the Queen visited Epsom. Silver ink-wells, made by a local craftsman in the shape of horses' hoofs, were presented to her. After attending the Derby, she went for a short walkabout by the Clock Tower, escorted by the Mayor (St John Heather). Seven years later she returned to open the shopping mall at the Ashley Centre.

205. This picture shows the crowd assembled outside Bromley Hurst, the old council offices at 33 Church Street, in September 1914. Patriotically responding to recruiting meetings and appeals, men poured into the town to enlist for military service. The recruits were carried off, in commandeered motorcars, to an Army Depot at Kingston.

1914~1919

On the pages which follow are short records of one hundred and six men of the parish of St Martin, Epsom, who fell in battle or died from wounds, or sickness in the Great War.

The Memorial Tablet on the North Wall of the Church tells their Names and Regiments and the Year and order of their death.

Twelve of their number were Sailors or Soldiers by profession, the others left home and calling, and those who held them dear, to join the Nation's Forces in the hour of her utmost need.

For their loyalty and the great sacrifice they made all are held in honour, and their memory is gratefully cherished, and handed down to those who shall follow after.

"Greater love hath no man than this, that a man lay down his life for his friends."

206. In July 1916 George V and Queen Mary visited the town. After lunch with Rosebery at The Durdans, they motored to Woodcote Park where they opened this tea and recreation room at the Convalescent Hospital. Later they visited over thirty wards at the County of London War Hospital, which had occupied the premises of Horton asylum for the duration of hostilities.

207. After the war came remembrance. A granite cross at the Ashley Road cemetery was unveiled in 1921 and the names of the fallen were added two years later. Plans for a memorial in the High Street were rejected by seven traders who had lost their sons and did not want to see a daily reminder.

208. Those who were disabled in the war were supported by the Lest We Forget Association: this 1932 photograph shows an entertainment for some of the members at the grandstand.

209. The 56th Surrey Home Guard (Epsom & Banstead) in 1941 – including Sgt. Alfred Smith of Lower Hill Road whose son wrote 'the formation of the Loyal Defence Volunteers found dad in his element and soon our dining-room was strewn with rifles and sub-machine guns as dad brought his homework home and stripped, cleaned and reassembled those weapons until he could do it in the dark blindfolded'.

210. The vicar of Epsom (C. R. Pattison Muir) offered prayers outside the new Town Hall in 1934. Lord Ebbisham, centrally placed before the double entrance doors, opened the building which – the press said – had cost 'a modest £33,000'. Slightly more was paid for the 1992 extension by H.L.M. Architects of Twickenham, which is intended to house 168 staff in open-plan offices around a central atrium.

211. Members of the council were preparing for the Third World War in 1954. Outside an artificial ruin on the site of Stone's brickyard, emergency cooking is in progress on an improvised hot plate cooking stove and the County Civil Defence Officer (beside the drainpipe chimney) explains her experimental work to the Mayor. The nuclear shelter, where council staff were supposed to remain while the London refugees panicked up Ashley Road towards the Downs, was demolished in 1990.

212. At 12 noon on 29 September 1937, His Majesty's Lieutenant of Surrey handed the Charter of Incorporation to Chuter Ede, the Charter Mayor. In reply, a loyal message to King George VI was read out and despatched by telegram. The Charter converted the Urban District of Epsom and Ewell (as it had been since 1933) into a Borough, but conferred no new rights or responsibilities. Nevertheless the 21st and 50th anniversaries of the Charter were greatly celebrated.

213 & 214.   On Sunday 25 June 1989 the Old Well on the Common was reopened. Mark Wilson, vicar of Christ Church, blessed it with holy water and the Mayor (Pam Ballard) joined the chairman of the Planning Committee (Mike Staples) in cutting ribbons at the entrance to the newly landscaped area. The Well now bears the following inscription:

The Epsom Well: The medicinal waters that in the 17th century made Epsom the first spa town in England, a great resort and famous throughout Europe.